Awakening to the knowing

of who you are;

ignites the flame of desire

for becoming

who you can truly be; at any

age!

Ready to take your dreams and goals
off that someday self?

Feel like a caged bird at times; anxious to fly?

Curious about discovering your own voice?

Eager to live your best, authentic self?

Anxious to step out on your own unique
path?

THEN THIS BOOK IS DEFINITELY
FOR YOU!

*****

PATRICIA LEONARD
'High Heel Shoes' Author

Need a motivational and entertaining speaker or seminar leader to inspire a group, organization or business unit? Check out Patricia's information and resources at:

www.PatriciaLeonard.net

patricia@patricialeonard.net

Books and Offerings by Patricia Leonard

Wearing High Heels In A *Flip Flop* World
The Listening And The Knowing...
The Now, How And Wow Of Success
'**Becoming Woman' Journal**
Happenings (Book Of Poetry)
Music DVD ('High Heel Shoes')

———————

I AM... (Spoken Word Album)

———————

RUNWAY TO SUCCESS
(Calendar Of Inspirational Messages)

———————

Hello Self... A Deck Of Motivational Cards

Patricia Leonard, President
www.patricialeonard.net
patricia@patricialeonard.net
615-406-9644

Sign up for podcasts and blogs at:
www.patricialeonard.net

Awakening to the knowing of
who you are;
ignites the flame of desire for
becoming
who you can truly be; at any age!

To contact the author:

patricia@patricialeonard.net
www.patricialeonard.net

ISBN: 978-0-9666797-9-3

Printed in the United States Of America

Book cover design by Rae Greenip
www.raegreenip.com

Author photo by Red Angle Photography
www.RedAnglePhotography.com

CONTENTS

ACKNOWLEDGEMENTS

This section gives recognition and 'thanks' to all who have walked with me during this lifetime and before, as they have contributed to my becoming. We each become more because of those who have crossed our path in some aspect of our living… and for that I am grateful.

Having said that; everyday God sends a blessing in some special way! And recently, the shower of blessings has doubled in my life; or maybe I am just paying more attention since starting this book.

After reaching out to my son and his wife who live in California, asking them to review the first 'rough' draft; their response brought tears to my heart. They generously offered their input from a younger generation's point of view and from a cultural and environmental diverse location.

Speaking of the differences in generations, cultures and geographic locations; a funny thing happened. My son and his wife inquired about the meaning of a term I had used in the book draft which immediately highlighted an obvious generational gap.

Their being of a younger generation and living on the west coast, reminded me, that perspectives and language are important to be considered in this writing. They, too, both inhabit the corporate world, are rearing a young family and have an appreciation for exposure across generations, cultures... and real life!

Grier, my son, has a degree in Journalism and works in the air quality control industry; Valerie has put her degree in Finance to work in a large corporation; their son, Gavin published a book at the age of six (*Gavin's World*) and their daughter, Gemma Rose is six and full of 'diva' energy.

They are a typical family exploring their own individual and family boundaries; and perfectly suited for providing input about this book and it's content; as the intention of the book is to focus on change and living a better quality of life for all regardless of age, social or cultural background.

We all know that what was yesterday; is not what is today! Their generosity in providing 'no charge' suggestions and impressions is appreciated.

Additionally, to all who have been part of my life journey to date, this acknowledgement section is for you, also. *I am... because of you!*

FOREWARD
To all things there is a beginning...

Funny thing; while sitting down at the computer to type the initial lines of this book; the question of what to say and how to say it suddenly surfaced as a roadblock to starting. Sometimes one's imagings and intentions seem to be misaligned with the act of doing. It was like something was there; yet, when attempting to articulate what it was, the words escaped me.

The reality of knowing and understanding self came to the forefront of my thinking at that moment. How could this lifelong relationship with self still be so unclear in really understanding me; since there had been so many journeys we have taken together.

Many questions began to come to mind... do others struggle with knowing who they are; is it difficult for other people to articulate an introduction to who they truly are, without uttering some title society has given them or at least one they have accepted themselves... because they really do not know who they are either?

My guess is that when asked who we are or asked to introduce ourselves, we often utter some string of nebulous words that really say little or nothing… or simply stand there dumb founded trying desperately to come up with an intelligent response. Then at last finally stating a few socially accepted ambiguous words to fill the space reserved for an answer to the question. Ever been there?

You may, at this moment, be questioning why you would even want to read a book written by someone who has a book titled *Hello, Self…* and yet, cannot determine what to say in the opening remarks about self or about the book title and contents.

Be patient, as knowing self is not about a 'one and done' process; my own living has taught me that! We will discover the contents as we journey together. We will learn more as we embark on the path ahead.

Life happens a day at a time! Think about it this way. Ever notice just when you get a glimpse of clarity about who you think you are, an unexpected personal action or behavior reveals something to the contrary; causing you to say, "What was that?" or "Who was that?"

Our past experiences and perceptions of those moments cause the unseen parts of us to reveal themselves. That is what makes living a journey and not a 'one and done' destination.

Every day is truly a new day, every experience is truly a new experience; every phase of life is truly a new encounter; even though most of us try to make it just like the one before. Until we can realize every moment of life is a new experience; we will miss the opportunity for true self awareness.

Life has shown me that there has seldom been a feeling of total confidence and certainty about what my actions would be or what the outcome would be, when stepping into a new commitment. Oh sure my approach is to have goals and make plans, and yet; life happens in the moment… not according to some well defined plan.

Someone, once wisely said, "all we have is the present moment and how we respond in that moment can and will impact the outcome, regardless of previously well defined planning. Living within a precisely formed and always predictable box would make life very boring… and could exclude the totality of what being human is really about… *that we have been given free choice*!

Some might say eliminating the partnership of the spiritual, mental, physical and emotional aspects from living might be defined as just surviving and not thriving. Agreed!

All things in life happen through a process of evolution even though we are only aware of that which we personally experience or see; and even with that, our eyes and emotions may hold biased perceptions.

So plans based upon our perceptions may not play out as we had hoped; however, the act of planning has the purpose of engaging us in a creative thinking process with a potential view of hoped for results. To take a step, if initially only in our planning mind, is so critical to progressing. Movement is motivating; stuckness is deflating!

So, my hope is that you will see this is only the initial learning; and a first step in discovering what *Hello, Self...* is about to reveal as we explore further.

However, I am confident each of you will make the discovery in your own particular way. Or another possible thought; if you decide to come along and be a self-discovery pioneer; perhaps you will offer myself (and others) your own personal learning process.

It is my suspicion we have both lived our lives in such a façade that to expect either of us to have a perfect clarity about who we truly are would be a ridiculous assumption.

Even the title *Hello, Self...* indicates that this is merely the introduction of two inner souls meeting. One that has been conditioned by the world it has inhabited; and the other that has often been denied self expression. These two inner souls make up each of us and often struggle to unite in a world that creates an environment of separateness.

That discovery would surely indicate that the initial introduction to self may bring more conversation, personal observation, occasional questioning, and even surface truths and emotional experiences that have been buried within.

It is my dream to create this book in such a way that it feels like a movie depicting discoveries of the reader's (your), inner most life and personal journey.

As a matter of fact, this book does not use chapters as dividers for topics; but frames as in a film. So, as you read the words in each frame, it is being suggested that you create a mind movie while reading, depicting you as the star and connecting with the words in such a way that parts of, or moments in your life, become visibly clear in your own mind's eye - as if you are watching yourself on a movie screen.

Actually, each of us has the responsibility of creating our own personal movie based upon the experiences we have in life and, of course, our perceptions of those experiences. Therefore, we truly are the star in our life movie; as well as, the script writer and director in defining how the story unfolds!

As you read the content shared, it may cause you to reflect on the choices you have made in the past; ask yourself *(without judgement)* "why you made those choices"; and maybe, even cause you to reflect more on editing future choices based upon your learning from past decisions you made along the way.

Of course, we both know we cannot go back and redo life...however, it may bring to light some special scenes from your life that can help in understanding the impact certain choices have had on your living...and cause you to choose to avoid walking down that same path again.

*"Our self-respect tracks our choices. Every time
we act in harmony with our authentic self and
our heart, we earn our respect. It is that simple.
Every choice matters."*
-Dan Coppersmith

Hello Self is an opportunity to change the frames in our movie for the future; by clarifying the messages we wish our living to exhibit; and by developing the star *(you)* in a role that celebrates your talents, makes transforming contributions and finds spaces for joy and happiness in your world.

*"Owning our story and loving ourselves through that
process is the bravest thing that we'll ever do."*
-Brené Brown

Hello Self is a chance to delete your old story and rewrite it based upon your present knowing. This book does not provide answers; you will furnish the data by exploring your authentic self and creating the screenplay for your award-winning life movie. Enjoy the path ahead; the path that few ever decide to travel!

Warmly,
Patricia

Your Cheerleader

THE TRAILER

Provoking your curiosity...

"Be a Voice; Not an Echo."
–Einstein

Recently, I ran across this quote by Albert Einstein, and decided to make it an opening to our journey of discovery. The words within the quote are definitely critical life elements and at the core of living a purposeful life.

Growing up in a household where children were to be seen and not heard was a challenge for me. Even as a small child my voice was used to speak my opinion; and not only for myself, but for others.

That attitude sometimes served me and other times it got me in a heap of trouble; however, it did not deter me from speaking my voice. It is my belief that 'being a voice' is about authenticity... and that authenticity is the best gift we can give ourself, and the best gift we can give others.

Having lived a lot of life and traveled down a multitude of roads in my coaching and speaking business; has revealed that many people are so diluted by societal expectations that they have no idea of who they are, what they stand for or what they want. And... rather than challenge that status quo living, many are often willing to accept what is dealt them... even if regret is the result.

We as individuals and a society are at another major crossroads, where being a voice is so critical to our futures. Over time, change has happened by those who dared to speak their heart and mind; and therefore, became a voice for change.

Looking around our world today, fear has seemed to water down most voices to nothing more than an echo for what is believed to be acceptable and the 'in thing'.

IT IS OBVIOUS NOW; THE SHIFT OF SELF DISCOVERY MUST BEGIN WITH YOU AND ME!

As an individual, if we let go of the need to fit in and chose to become a voice; we can inspire others to do the same; and make a significant impact in our families, communities and in the world. The shift begins with you and me.

But your initial question may be, "how can I begin?" Well, years ago while searching for 'me' my personal moto emerged (*see below*) and has continued to be my guide in living. Of course, you will find your own motto or guiding quote.

"I walk between the raindrops in life; I'm letting nothing rain on my parade."

With more and more confusion and hostility in our world, we need individuals, leaders and organizations inspiring cooperation versus competition; creating inclusion, not division; encouraging, valuing and finding middle ground for win-win outcomes. Sounds easy, right? Well, if it is so easy, we are not doing a great job of such a seemingly easy task.

It appears the echoes are louder and more powerful than the voices. Is that lack of speaking up driven from no clear personal focus, not wanting to make waves or just wanting to fit in and be accepted by those with titles of power? How about you? Are you speaking up; and if not 'WHY'?   Ask yourself that question!

Speaking of the impact of titles and power; why is it that some speak up to gain control and power over others; instead of raising the power of all?   After having asked myself that question it came to me that it may be summed up in something that could be identified as critical ego theory (CET).

The need for control and acceptance is a very powerful motivator in a transitioning society, culture and world community. What is really needed at such a time, is more individuals and leaders being willing to become a voice for empowerment, cooperation, collaboration and resolution. These are key elements of strengthening a world and its people. And, yes, it begins with you and me.

With more ego centered thinking in the world today, finding middle ground resolutions for win-win outcomes is getting more difficult; resulting in ineffective progress. It appears the echoes are louder and more powerful than the voices. If that is true, what may be driving that lack of speaking up?

Our society seems to think that repeating something heard is considered voicing a platform. Truthfully that is simply the echoing of a message heard and repeated; often without a clear understanding of the meaning. The value and impact of repeating words without a heartfelt connection are just taking up empty space without feeling, commitment or value-added impact. The power of voice is heard by constructing a message from one's own values and world view; not just echoing what another has already stated... and often stated without definition or understanding.

Over time, change has happened by those who dared to speak their heart and mind; and therefore, become a voice for change. From a general observation of our world today, as stated previously, it appears fear has diluted most voices to nothing more than an echo of what is believed to be acceptable and the 'in thing'.

We as individuals and a society are at a crossroads, where being a constructive and impactful voice is so critical to our individual and global futures. And as earlier pointed out, the shift begins with you... and me!

Obviously, Einstein's quote was not about just fitting in; but speaking from one's own core! The message behind the quote, suggested finding one's authentic voice and having the courage to use it. Those willing to come from their authentic self do not concern themselves with popularity; as they are more concerned with being authentic and having a positive impact.

Without personal conviction one's voice can become polluted by those using power and control to encourage or force a renouncement of their position. Our response must be firm, but we must, also, remain humble in our resolve; keeping an open ear to other's point of view and thought.

The key objective of this section is to emphasize the knowing of one's inner motives and values; then speak from that knowing. This clarity starts by first getting to know self and being honest with self.

It is at this point that we will begin the journey to discovering and reclaiming our authentic voice. Enjoy the journey ahead.

_____

ILLUSIONS - A passage from the book by Richard Bach, seems to enhance the closing of the trailer.

You are led through your lifetime

by the inner learning creature,

the playful spiritual being

that is your real self.

> **Don't turn away from possible futures**
>
> **before you're certain you don't have**
>
> **anything to learn from them.**

HELLO AND WELCOME
A single 'hello' could lead to a million 'hello moments.'

Several years ago, Patricia Leonard & Associates, was created with the goal of making an impact in the quality of life for all people. My intention was to build a business that created avenues for individuals to feel free to explore, express and execute their dreams and goals.

It has definitely been an evolving process of learning more about myself; while uncovering the layers of past experiences, self-limiting beliefs, social impacts and fear of failures.

These personal insights, learnings and conversations with self, have led me to write this book... as it has become my belief and discovery that these moments of awareness are not unique to just me.

Hello Self... is clearly the starting point where a purposeful life and a passion-driven career begin. All dreams, desires and goals actually originate in the imagination prior to our taking action on them.

While action and forward movement are important; it is the alignment of passion and purpose that brings long-term satisfaction. Moving forward or taking action without clarity can result in a spin-zone of 'action without satisfaction'.

And, as all things in life are continually evolving, it is critical to re-introduce self to self at various phases in life. We are not static beings.

Hello Self... can be a wakeup call for individuals and businesses, in numerous stages of transition, to re-evaluate the status regularly, and engage in what might be thought of as 'imagine thinking' (imagine if ...thinking)? This creative thinking process offers an opportunity to step outside a typical pattern of thought to bring in new flashes of insight and possibility. These are the moments that can offer a deeper evaluation of personal, business, societal and cultural impacts.

My own living and my work have taught me the importance of checking in with self regularly; as my life experiences and career transitions shift it. This checking in requires an assessment of personal happiness, goal accomplishments and future commitments. The key purpose of this personal review is intended to improve the possibility of a more fulfilled quality of life.

On a scale from one to five where would you rate your personal and career happiness at this time in your life? Choose the number that best describes your answer and jot a couple of notes to yourself as to 'why' that rating.

PERSONAL   1   2   3   4   5

CAREER   1   2   3   4   5

And, as the global world has recently experienced a major disruption resulting in the crumbling and/or transitioning of familiar systems and structures; we must look outside self at 'what was' and re-think and re-assemble our beliefs, perspectives and views on 'what is' next in bringing personal and professional happiness.

This dramatic shift can result in setting individuals free to look outside their accepted box called 'life' and create a true heart centered awakening. These dynamic external factors may be the catalyst necessary to ignite the heart and soul of a society of individuals to now explore more of who they are, who they can be and what they desire from life. The transition requires knowing more about who we are from a mental, emotional and behavioral standpoint.

Daniel Goleman, an American psychologist introduced the idea of something called emotional intelligence (otherwise known as emotional quotient or EQ) as the ability to understand, utilize, and manage one's own emotions in positive ways to relieve stress, communicate effectively, empathize with others, overcome challenges and defuse conflict.

The five categories of EQ are identified below:

- **Self-awareness**-*you know how you're feeling, acting, and appearing.*

- **Self-regulation**-*the ability to remain calm in emotionally trying situations.*

- **Motivation**-*the internal ability and drive to do what needs to be done.*

- **Empathy**-*you're good at intuiting what other's feelings might be.*

- **Social skills**-*ability to recognize social cues and communicate with others.*

Using This Emotional Intelligence in Life by...

- Being able to accept criticism and responsibility.

- Being able to move on after making a mistake.

- Being able to say 'no' when you need to.

- Being able to share your feelings with others.

- Being able to solve problems in ways that work for everyone.

- Having empathy for other people.

- Having great listening skills.

The brief definition insertion is intended to help explain and validate the importance of the *Hello, Self...* personal awareness mission we are taking on.

Hello, Self... opens the door to exploration, re-defining and a re-aligning of self. Having discovery conversations with self can open new doors revealing who we may have become, while we were busy adjusting to old beliefs, habits and accepted cultural norms; that truly may be outdated in this emerging new society.

What may start as an unplanned conversation with self, might just end up being a positive life changing event. A significant *Hello, Self...* moment; if you will!

Hello, Self... acknowledges that everyday we are a new person; however, for most part we assume, we know who we are and seldom feel the need to get to know who we have become. The eastern culture sees each day as a new beginning; while we see it, for most part, as a continuation of the day before; or living in a status quo state. With that mindset; we assume we already know self, fail to reconnect and finally lose complete contact.

Hello, Self... interestingly aligns with my own **motivating and accountability style of encouraging and empowering myself and others**. With this book, it is my mission to expand visions, build runways to success and encourage celebration by inspiring you, my readers, to get excited about turning your cants into cans and your dreams into plans; through a process of inviting and embracing more *Hello, Self...* moments.

Expect the unexpected to be revealed to you and about you as you make a commitment to build a partnering relationship with the real you!

Hello, Self...
Alas, two souls are living in my breast,
And one wants to separate itself from the other.
One holds fast to the world with earthly passion
And clings with twining tendrils:
The other lifts itself with forceful craving
To the very roof of heaven.

*...Goethe, writing in Faust,
provides a poetic description of
the two souls living within us;
one that acts regardless of the outcome,
and the other that clings to the world of
fear, and dies wondering.*

OVERVIEW
Sneak peek...

LET'S BEGIN HERE BY BRIEFLY DEFINING HELLO, SELF... MOMENTS, EVENTS or HAPPENINGS...

Then Share Some Specific
Hello, Self... Stories.

Hello, Self... moments can happen when we let go of the negative messages we give ourselves about not having enough money, going alone would be too risky, bringing up fears about the 'what if's' that might happen or telling ourselves we lack the talents required. Those type of conversations to self can limit one's personal and professional happiness and experiences.

These are some of the key reasons *Hello, Self...* is such a critical process. We can discover and release the power of the soul by taking the time to engage in conversations of empowerment from our inner

---

spiritual source which are often more positive than those from the mind or the ego.

As a way to set the scene for the contents of this book/movie it may make sense to share some real life experiences from others who have published their *Hello, Self...* happenings or stories in articles; some who have been interviewed about how they got where they are today; and still others who have shared in group conversations about unexplainable encounters and unusual moments that impacted their lives significantly.

These sharings may not have been titled *Hello, Self...*moments by those individuals who shared them or those shared by the reporters who shared the stories... however they all agreed that there was a moment they called their 'wakening' or awareness moment. In this writing we are calling those times *Hello, Self...* moments, in order to highlight their practical and social relevance in our lives and to align with the intention of this book/movie. Following are some of those stories.

STORY ONE

As a small girl, I recall my mother telling me about a time when she was trying to make a life changing decision. After posing the question many times to herself; she remained in a spin zone of going over and over the possible consequences relating to her decision. Then she said something unusual happened.

While standing in the living room of her home, all of a sudden experiencing a very strange feeling of something that felt like it was running down over her body; the feeling started at the top of her head and went down to the bottom of her feet.

It was at that time, the answer became clear. She felt confident about making the decision; even though the final outcome was still questionable.

Sometimes, life requires us to trust the nudges or quiet whispers even though we do not know the meaning of them or the outcome; we simply need to trust it is for our best and highest good.

"Do not be afraid to travel a new path; It may be the way to find what you've been looking for all along." ~ Anonymous

STORY TWO

A 2021 article about, John Voight telling Tucker Carlson, a radio host, about a low-level time in his life and what happened.

He said he was going through a divorce; career was in the pot and in his little house he found himself on the floor at wits end and saying out loud… "it's just too hard." It was at that very moment he heard a voice whispering in his ear saying the words… 'that's the way it is supposed to be'.

"What was that" he questioned to himself, but there was no response, however; he felt the dark depression lift. Next morning, he got up full of energy and jokingly turned on the radio and the first message he heard was 'take another step today' and that message had such an impact.

He said, he realized that we are to get up each day and do something meaningful… so from now on he says, he gets up every day and says "God …so what do you have for me today." John admitted it was a life changing moment; and, yes, life still happens, he says!

———————

"Just one small positive thought in the morning can change your whole day."
-Dalai Lama

STORY THREE

Another story from a Tucker Carlson interview was with Rick Santorum. Mr. Santorum and his wife, learned two weeks prior to the birth of their baby; that the child would have problems. As they have strong faith, they decided that God's gift is to be cherished and their son lived for 2 hours.

His wife, Karen, kept writing letters about that experience and the impact it had made on their lives. Finally, she was encouraged by her mom to create a book of those letters and the book sold over 5K copies.

———————

To all things there is a purpose.

———————

"The difference between a flower and a weed is judgement."
-Unknown

STORY FOUR

A story from a BUZZ FEED online article shared by **Kylie M.** After graduating college, I was working in fashion public relations and at the same time having a "quarter-life" crisis.

I remember being on my hands and knees shoving a too-small shoe onto a model's foot, and tore a bow off the shoe. Some people acted like the world was ending—I simply superglued it back on. But at that moment, I realized that I needed a change: Why on Earth was I working in this industry if I didn't have the passion for it?

I had always cooked… in the past it was my creative outlet, a way of decompressing after a long day; but I never saw it as a career path. **It wasn't until I was writing down all the recipes I had created over the years as a Christmas present for my mom, that I realized working with food was my true passion**.

That remembering 'aha' instant led me to creating my food blog, <u>Cooking with Cocktail Rings</u>; and I love every minute… the recipes, the narrative, the photography.

"Following my dream and doing something I love has made all the difference."

———

"Everyone has been made for some particular work, and the desire for that work has been put in every heart."
-Rumi

STORY FIVE

Another story from my personal life. My nail and toenail manicure kit, after use, is and has always been stored in a zipped toiletry bag in my bathroom cabinet under the sink. Recently, needing the clippers and file and going to the usual storage spot, only to discover, that the toiletry bag was there; but the clippers were missing.

Since there is only me in the house, it was not plausible for me to blame anyone else for using them and not putting them back! It would have been an easy out; but it forced a conversation with self… which frankly got a little frustrating and self-blaming.

After racking my brain, over and over with questions, as to where they could be; or where I might have laid them; then finally asking myself the direct question, "Patricia, where did you put those clippers." The answer came in a knowing rather than specific words revealing to me that they were under the sink. But I knew better as I always zipped the bag when finished, so it was impossible for anything to fall out.

After no clippers and no other clues; finally surrendering to the possibility that they were in my bathroom cabinet under the sink. Then getting down on my hands and knees; and peeking over the hairspray and shampoo containers… guess what I found lying behind the containers? Yes, much to my surprise, the missing clippers were laying behind those hairspray containers!!!

The finding still amazed me as to how that item came out of the zipped bag; but, finally had to confess to the reality, that it did. Call it intuition or just plain luck, at last the mystery was finally solved.

And, looking back, it impressed on me the fact that maybe, just maybe, when inquiring with self about life questions or decisions, it may be valuable to pay attention to the nudges, whispers or knowing's that come from our inner self, as they could prove beneficial.

Funny thing, that experience is now causing me to recall other times of having misplaced my cell phone or car keys... with the same results. Maybe trusting that inner knowing could be a powerful tool and 'stress buster'. Perhaps you should try it, too! What do you have to lose?

"Following intuition allows decision and action to be made in the same instant."
-Maria Erving

STORY SIX

During a conversation with my accountant following a tax filing appointment, she let me know that she was retiring that year.

She had run her own successful CPA business for many years; and of course, with my interest in what drives one's specific wake up or *Hello, Self...* decision moments; I inquired about her 'why' for closing the business in this particular year.

She shared the story about recently losing her husband and her sister in the same year which caused her to have an intimate conversation with self about the dreams and goals she had yet to be lived. Those conversations, made her realize that life comes with no guarantees.

She shared that her decision immediately became clear; it was time to retire and live the life she is now dreaming of.

"Life happens and dreams fade; unless we act on commitments made."

I Promise!

STORY SEVEN

Actually, now thinking about more *Hello, Self...* stories from my own life, here is another example. Over a period of nearly three years, my dream of going to Italy had became a constant conversation and affirmation with self. The culture, fashion, incredible artists, architectural achievements and savory food continually occupied my imaginings.

And, it seemed I was seeing Italian reminders all around me.

Anyway, one day while reading my FaceBook messages, there was a post by an individual who had lead a workshop I had attended a year earlier. The message was an offer to use their international timeshare for a visit to either, Italy or Brazil. My curiosity caused me to inquire more about the potential catch.

To my surprise, there was no catch and the 10-day visit to Italy cost me just about $2000.00 for the entire trip. Unbelievable! It was an experience of a lifetime...and everything that had existed in my previous dreaming. Just another *Hello, Self...* experience proving the power of positively speaking our wishes and desires to the inner self; with commitment!

How does it all happen by just a desire spoken out loud? I really do not know; however, I know it happens. And, this is not my only experience of such an event in my life... and probably in yours! And, yes it is true that our subconscious self is not a sorting machine; like the conscious self.

The subconscious self hears what is said or requested, and acts. That can be for our highest good or for whatever we are saying to self. So be careful what you say… your subconscious self is listening!

STORY EIGHT – YOUR STORY

My bet is that you are now recalling several such moments in your own life where you have conscientiously or unconsciously come up with a solution through a conversation with self… or a gut feeling happened… or you saw a road sign that triggered an idea… or you woke up in the middle of the night with the answer… or…!

Well, it is time for you to now jot down a note or two about your own significant story or stories…that you are now recalling from your life.

My Personal Hello, Self… story, stories or moments…

And it is my suggestion, that you do this as an acknowledgment to your inner knowing.

Patricia Leonard

At this minute; you may be saying to yourself that you do not remember any such moments like that in your life or have the time to write them down, even if you did remember.

Well, that attitude is exactly why we all struggle to find our own voice and choose instead to remain an echo. We do not take the time to pay attention, acknowledge or listen to the nudges, knowings or proddings of self.

The value of starting with a few stories from others and suggesting you might recall and pen your own experience(s); is intended to prime the pump of possibility for building a listening relationship with that inner-self part of you!

Creating that relationship and commitment is critical to the goals of this book/movie and the concept of *Hello, Self...*

AND IN, EXPERIENCING A MEANINGFUL AND PURPOSEFUL LIFE!

Now go get your popcorn and soda; then set back in a comfortable chair, as the first frame of this book/movie is about to begin.

Hello, Self...

Frame One...

THE AWARENESS

"There are two great days in a person's life, the day we are born and the day we discover why."

-William Barclay

FRAME ONE of this book movie, 'yes book/movie'; per an earlier stated intention. The book/movie approach has been chosen to engage you and your interest in more than just reading words. It suggests a deeper involvement from you by playing in a starring role.

By setting the stage in this manner it is focused on attracting your interest and understanding, as if you are watching a movie where you are stepping into and out of the scenes occasionally.

So, let's begin frame one with a quick review of a book by Tony Woodlief, titled *"I, Citizen: A Blueprint for Reclaiming American Self-Governance".*

His book is about reclaiming American self-governance, where he suggests that because each of us are becoming less connected and involved with each other in our families and communities; our country is asking for trouble within.

With that awareness of 'I Citizen' *(you),* have a responsibility to be a key part of not only self awakening; but contributing to and engaging the world in awakening. This is a key role of the *Hello, Self...* concept.

Hello Self... suggests that making an impact requires self-awareness first. This knowing and self-awareness encourages personal action and contribution which can potentially create a rippling effect of outward influence.

Hello, Self... *acknowledges that each individual is unique and has their own future to discover and create. Awakening to that knowledge can empower self.*

Hello, Self... *is a sharing for all, about becoming aware of one's previous commitment to wearing a mask of society norms, accepting limited beliefs about self and having hidden that knowing within!*

Hello, Self... *is about the moment you finally realize your value and your talents, and truly fall in love with self.*

Hello, Self... *is to recognizing those moments in our lives that may come masked as synchronistic happenings, risk taking events or just the ripple of results from saying 'yes' to the suggestion of a friend.*

Hello, Self... *does not intend to compare one person or one community of people against another. It is about self-discovery, self-monitoring and self-awareness (mindfulness) of*

something intellectually does not automatically make it happen in one's daily living.

Many of us are living under the illusion of how it is supposed to happen based upon the writings and teachings of someone else; and giving little attention to the thoughts and emotions of self. Our personal process of living is often invisible to each of us.

Hello, Self... is being offered as a way of making the invisible visible!

Authors and coaches sell books and collect coaching fees *(and, I am an author, speaker and coach)* convincing you that they did their self-discovery success in a one 'three step' or 'five step' process; and all magically happened as they had originally dreamed.

AND, let me remind you of a magical paradise that is for sale, if you buy that statement. Self-discovery and self-mastery are part of a lifelong process... requiring removing our self-protecting masks of denial and becoming truthful with self.

"To accomplish great things, we must not only act, but also dream; not only plan, but also believe."
-Anatole France... A French Poet In 1800-1900

Hello, Self...

Frame Three...
THE BEGINNING

So, you may now be asking; where and how does one begin this getting-to-know self process? After all, once you have introduced yourself to self, by saying *Hello, Self...* what happens next? Great question, right? Well, here we go!

FRAME THREE is taking the platform setting of the two prior frames and creating a connection through action. By now, you have more than likely been saying to yourself that it is time to move on and have been wondering when all this previous talking would transition into walking and getting on with it!

That is often how we all respond when we are ready for a transition; we just want to jump in and get going. While it is great to be excited about getting out of the rut of one's present lifestyle; it is equally as important to understand 'WHY' we want out and 'WHY' we are so anxious to jump into something else.

What makes the 'WHY' so important for us to know? Simon Oliver Sinek, is a British-American author and inspirational speaker. In his book titled *Start with Why*; he says that the 'WHY' is the key motivator in keeping us on track with our commitments.

That is especially true when things don't go as originally planned or happen as fast as we had expected. And, remembering the 'WHY' can be the catalyst for moving forward when the entire road seems to be filled with potholes and detours.

But before jumping in it is good to establish the moving forward groundwork by having some personal *Hello, Self...* conversations.

It is not, and this book/movie is not, just about following a step-by-step strategy from an a-list author's book, on the market, that guarantees you the success of becoming a millionaire, or some famous celebrity if only you do these three things.

Hello, Self... is a life process that first begins by becoming honest with self now and throughout the various phases of your life and living!

Regardless, of what many consultants and coaches may tell you, life is not a linear undertaking; where you will arrive by simply first doing one certain thing, then another certain thing; and that will get you the clarity and the result in all you have ever dreamed of.

So, since we are all often looking for a quick fix to life, you may be, again, getting impatient about when this book's impactful content will ever begin.

Well, surprise it has already begun!!! And the fact that you are still reading, you are already engaged in experiencing a process for learning more about who you are.

If you are more curious and maybe a bit frustrated about where this is going... that is a perfect time for you to start a *Hello, Self...* conversation. If what you are experiencing is your typical behavior when you are not clear or not told the next steps; perhaps finding your 'WHY' for those feelings, might offer some insights to who you are when approaching other aspects of your life that seem out of your control. You are the one to determine that 'WHY'!

Oh! While we are in this 'WHY' discussion; it seems a perfect time to have a conversation with self as to why you have chosen to pick up this book to browse, at this time in your life.

Is it because you are curious about the meaning of the title; feeling a need to get out of your comfort zone; entering a major turning point in your life; starting over and wanting to begin with a clean slate or some other key reason?

Interestingly enough, there are various reasons why many of us read books... we are often looking for answers or an escape from our present situation or state of being.

Living life is a journey in an unfamiliar forest with nothing but trees in every direction. An out of control feeling or knowing coming from our fears or egos may cause one to do something even if it may not be in their best interest.

If this is true for you, you are not alone, as that is exactly how most of us live our lives. Just tell me what the quick fix is so I can get on with making it happen! When that happens, relax and breathe as those moments can be the perfect time to have a conversation with self about the truth behind the frustration or uneasy feelings.

Even after saying all that, if quick fixes are your style… the next paragraphs are about quick fixes you might be tempted to jump into immediately… then research and purchase my second book (*yet to be written*) in a series of **Hello, Self…** books focused on more quick fixes and 100 percent perfect answers!

Why do I know that quick fixes are what you had hoped for by this point in the book/movie? We are both human and have traveled down those same roads of exploration, frustration and self doubt; hoping for an answer. And to be honest; just because we write about life does not mean we are experts... like you; authors, consultants and speakers are learning about life and living it as we go.

A line from John Michael Montgomery's song titled, Life's a Dance says it best...

"Life's a dance we learn as we go... sometimes we lead; sometimes we follow."

While learning to dance with life we may discover that we have two left-feet, forget the right step count and move like a robot in undiscovered territory. So, an applause goes out to you for simply picking up this book and reading the previous pages of content, even if you decide at this point to lay it back down.

However, it is my hope that there has been enough curiosity raised in the previous pages that you will be enticed to stay for the remainder of the frames.

In life it is so easy to watch others enjoying the dance; but still choose to be a wallflower because of fear and lack of trust in self... then miss the joy of the dance by choosing to go home early. Will you decide to stay for the dance?

You obviously have an interest in dancing with life as a way of meeting your real self, and discovering that we are all more alike than we are different; regardless of age, gender, ethnicity, education or economic status. Since meeting you briefly, it is my hope that you will decide to dance and take me as your partner in experiencing the various aspects of this book/movie .

"If life were predictable it would cease to be life, and be without flavor."
-Eleanor Roosevelt

Okay, it's time to get out on the dance floor and begin discovering the 'WHY' one should even bother with this idea of self-knowing! Let's dance; I will lead in this dance.

———————

Tim McGraw reminds us in his book titled:

GRIT & GRACE

*"That taking ownership
is the first step in
creating a different kind
of relationship with yourself."*

Hello, Self...

Frame Four...

THE VIEW

FRAME FOUR of this book/movie highlights that there is something happening in our world and life today; yet, it keeps us in the dark questioning exactly what it is and the possible impacts. Isn't that how movies engage their audience?

They keep the viewer in suspense about the outcome in order to intensify their curiosity about what to expect in the remaining frames. And all the while, we as the audience are trying to predict what happens next; just as we do in our own lives. It seems we are torn between the wanting to know and the surprise of not knowing!

Your own uncertainty may even be surfacing some question, such as:

- Will the remaining frames bring more clarity to all the questions about this obviously transitory time the world is facing; and, what self-awareness has to do with it?

- Does being part of a WOKE society mean that there is an awareness already happening at the core level of humanity?

- Is this metamorphosing period that is rippling outward into the world impacting all existing systems, structures and processes?

- If it is a wakeup movement for humanity; what is the driver or drivers of this transition and waking up period?

- What possible impact could a single person have on addressing change in a universal shift?

- Is this hyper interest in global metamorphosis just a façade created by a segment of the world that are bored and feel disconnected?

- Have we as a global world and society been at a similar point during our maturing?

- Is there hope for a positive future ... who is creating the roadmap; or is there a roadmap?

Even more possible questions may be: Is the key driver about global warming? Is it about a health pandemic? Or about a nation of people with unrecognized common goals, adrift on a sea of confusion, trying to access a utopia conjured up in creative (*maybe even destructive*) minds? Or is it a re-positioning time in preparation for an entirely new human experience?

Each of you may have a differing opinion or response as to the real driver or drivers. We could take the view that it is a general happening in all of society. Or another possibility is that certain segments of society are the key drivers and others are caught up in the wake; or perhaps another segment is totally lost and just going along for the ride.

And yet, regardless of how we divide it, society is made up of individuals expressing diverse viewpoints. So, whether we view the world in groups or as individuals, the transformation taking place has similarities in all scenarios.

Let's take a macro unscientific view at what is happening by dividing this movement into three general societal groups; then look at the three groups from an individual standpoint.

GROUP NUMBER ONE - *one third of all people in our society are asking for a chance to get back to normal; normal being defined as the place where familiar and standard operations are the daily way of life. They are wishing for a sense of security and comfort in knowing the happenings that can be expected in their day-to-day lives.*

GROUP NUMBER TWO – *another third of the population is trying to fit into this newly divided and disruptive way of life, by having one foot in the familiar and the other foot in the emerging unknown. This place creates a sense of vulnerability and out of control feeling; causing stress and unrest. This stress and unrest provides a breeding ground for fear, illness, separation, fighting, survival, looting, rioting and destruction, in general.*

GROUP NUMBER THREE - *The final one-third or the WOKE group is trying to redefine society in their own terms by creating a new space for emotions and biases to reside; while tossing out all* *the existing systems, structures and processes.*

It seems, that in their minds, the world has to start all over in an attempt to create a more perfect global society. (No specific details, however, have been identified as to how to do this; just destroy all that exists presently... and figure out the new while in forward movement; regardless of the destruction in the process).

While this group is trying to define their role, they may be creating movements based on emotion and separateness rather than, pragmatically engaging or even acknowledging diverse viewpoints for discussion and consensus building.

Viewing these segments from the ***Hello, Self...*** approach may best be defined and understood in this business model introduced by Dr. Stephen Covey years ago, which he tagged as the 'Circles of Influence'.

A graphic of Dr. Covey's model is shown on the following page.

Influences

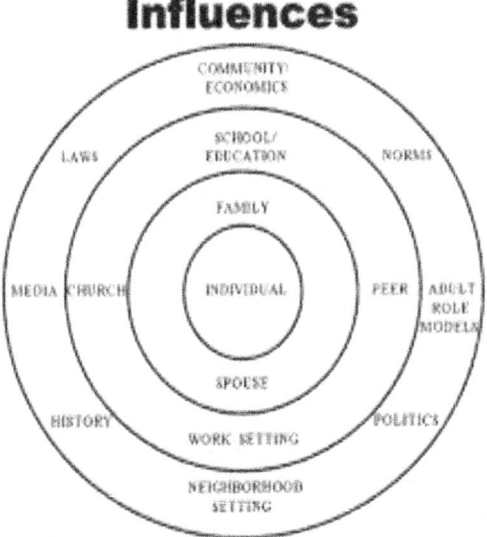

Dr. Covey's, model is a series of circles suggesting that the inner most circle is about the individual and the true starting point in personal, community and societal transition.

Without clarity of one's morals and beliefs, or a society's core values and principles; it is easy to take action based upon emotions frustration and competition. That approach is often ineffective in manifesting a positive outcome in our own life or the lives of those in the outer circles.

This lack of accomplishment or progress can lead to personal disappointment and a feeling of inadequacy. His model demonstrates that impactful transformative thinking always begins at the core of the matter.

Until we understand our own motives and behaviors we cannot effectively contribute, impact change or make a difference within ourselves or other elements of society which are identified in the outer circles.

That inner work is where the transition begins; and it is the work of *Hello, Self...* at an individual level! This model begins to respond to some of the questions highlighted earlier in this frame.

We typically look for answers outside self; and, yet, Dr.Covey suggests that regardless of the size of the transition affecting us and our piece of the world; it must first begin with us knowing ourselves by assessing self and our own personal beliefs, values, motivators and behaviors. Creating this relationship with self can be helpful in setting in place ongoing mindful practices... consequently, rippling outward to impact possible change in others and in the affected environment.

As the world changes, truths change. Be willing to be curious and willing to accept the conclusions that your senses provide, even if they contradict hard won beliefs within you. Being inquisitive and open to learning new perspectives are critical to a transitory process at the individual, family, community, society and/or global level.

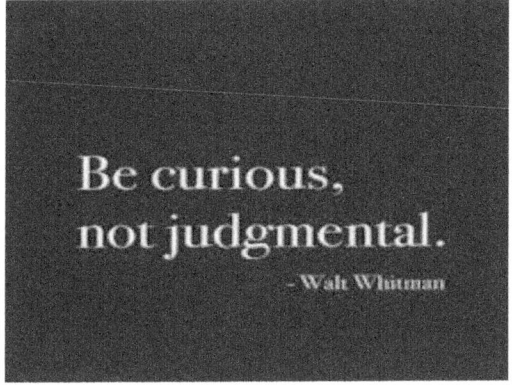

Hello, Self...

Frame Five...
THE AWAKENING

FRAME FIVE begins to highlight the possibility of what breakthrough moments can offer. First of all there is no one right way to begin discovering the totality of who one is, regardless of what others may tell us. There are multiple ways to begin to discover the authentic self, as we have been saying in previous parts of this book/movie.

Some may approach beginning through a bible study group, others like reading another person's story of their beginnngs or life journey; still another group may become clear during a catastrophic life or health event; and some may even say they experienced a revelation or awakening moment and truly cannot explain what happened or put the specifics of it into words.

External sources can, also, be an awakening vehicle, either by plan or by accident. Losing a job; facing the loss of a family member or friend; seeking counseling after deciding to leave an abusive relationship; being shocked by a catastrophic weather event; experiencing betrayal by a business partner; or facing an unexplainable spiritual awakening moment; just to mention a few.

Another thought is that a mother or father may be open and honest with a sibling about a wake up moment in their life (*favorable or unfavorable*) that shifted their personal direction. These are all samples of life events and experiences that may have changed one's life. These are just a few examples and you may have others you have personally experienced or you can think of.

Truly, the 'how' to awaken to the inner self is not the most significant piece of the beginning. The most important piece is making the decision to find peace, happiness and fulfillment in life; then doing something about it. That decision initiates the transition!

So, the right way to begin is just simply CHOOSING to begin; and start by observing self in everyday living without making excuses for any thoughts, actions or behaviors... simply observing them.

Perhaps, even initiating a conversation with self about the observations might be helpful, too. As, those thoughts and actions may be behaviors we have become accustomed to, inherited or accepted as just the way it is.

We are often unaware of the thoughts we have or the words we speak. Words or messages such as; 'I am not', 'I should', 'he/she is smarter', 'I could not', 'I am not lucky', or 'If I had'... 'they have rich parents', 'he is just lucky', 'she has no talent; she is just good looking'... whether verbalized or thought about can become self-fulfilling prophecies.

Such dialogue or thoughts to self about self, sends a disempowering message. It is not really our intent to delegitimize self; it has often simply become a habit of self-talk.

A self-help guru once said, that when we do slip up *(and, we will)* and say something that could send a message to or about self that is not empowering; we need to cancel it out by simple saying 'cancel, cancel'. The intention of saying 'cancel cancel' is to stop the negative or depowering words or statements to be canceled before rippling out into the universal ethers.

To become aware, through *Hello, Self...* observations and conversations, is not a one and done event; as has been previously mentioned. Some call this process of becoming aware, MINDFULNESS. Practicing mindfulness is about paying attention, in the moment, to what we do and what we say... to self, to others and about self and others.

But regardless of the fancy names or process titles, it is simply paying attention to our thoughts, behaviors and actions in the moment of living them. AND, it is important to stress that, simply paying attention to the processes of the inner and outer self, in the moments of living, is not easy; as most of us operate on automatic much of the time.

The belief's we carry around about self is key. If you see yourself as a victim, you will no doubt blame others for your behaviors, lack of opportunities, problems or the choices you have had to make throughout your life.

The excuses we sight are most often outside our personal self, such as: I grew up in a disfunctional family, my life is like this because of my social upbringing, I didn't or don't have the money, my physical disability has inhibited my success; or a multitude of other situations we decide are the culprits.

DON'T PLAY THE VICTIM
TO CIRCUMSTANCES
YOU MAY HAVE CREATED!

EXCUSES CAN KEEP YOU A PRISONER
TO YOUR BELIEFS!

These views and reasonings are only our attempts to validate the behaviors, thoughts and excuses we have for the way we respond to life; and for feeling no sense of personal responsibility.

Once we wake up to this victim reality about ourselves, there is a discovery of the possible impact to our personal happiness and professional success.

THE DISCOVERY;
A BEHIND THE FAÇADE VIEW...

The avoidance of taking responsibility for our actions and becoming aware is a way to keep hiding behind a façade of being a victim in our family, workplace and society... then accepting that this is the way it is. After all, it is the lifestyle that validates one's victimhood mentality and actually feels familiar.

A lifestyle of trying to fit in and be accepted; hiding behind a wall of safety and security; repeating the accepted societal language; stuffing emotions and feelings; and/or choosing lifestyles and friends based upon economic and cultural status becomes our superficial appearance or illusion... we call living.

> *"Make yourselves sheep,*
> *and the wolves will eat you."*
> -Ben Franklin said in 1773

Some choose to live within these self-inflicted boundaries just to feel a part of an in-group. Many times, it is seen as a way to avoid conflict; even though, it may lead to inner strife, low self-esteem and a life without purpose... while the outward view may seem like, to others, they are living the ideal human experience.

Speaking of the invisible inner strife we can experience, reminds me of the lyrics to a song I wrote, titled 'Tears of the Heart'. The lyrics make the point that tears of the heart are not visible. Sad, but it is the truth about so many who have chosen to sell themselves short and become 'sheep'!

We all become such great pretenders at playing these many deceptive roles; that others actually become envious of how well put together we are; while inside a storm is brewing. What are some of the roles you play in your life movie just to be accepted, to fit in, or to hide behind? It is more than likely we all have some areas of our lives where we deny ourself full expression; either out of fear or lack of confidence.

What are some possible examples to help in your thinking: saying yes to a boss when we actually want to say "take this job and shove it"; admitting to another that you have a fear of being able to do the job you have just accepted; noticing someone taking credit for the work of another, without even flinching as they say it; listening to an associate who constantly touts their accomplishments when you know how it really happened; or feeling inadequate when transitioning into a new family role… (*my personal example on the next page*).

My self admitting moment… remembering when I became Mom Pat, a grandmother for the first time.

I struggled with being the kind of grandmother, previously witnessed by others as examples. 'Gaga-Gugu' was not my style.

Finally, after several personal conversations with self, I finally accepted me; And, funny thing, so did my family.

Then there are those who have followed their own hearts and dreams regardless of the existing state of affairs or societal expectations; and may have been seen as rebels, renegades or mavericks. They are viewed or may have been viewed as pushing the limits of disruption; even though a part of them may have kept one foot in a safe area.

They are often those individuals who may be called 'straddlers'; walking with one foot in what is familiar, accepted or popular; and the other foot on the edge of rebellion, defiance and disruption. These are inventors, creators of movements to improve, and/or filmmakers or authors with a goal of expanding possibility thinking through a story message.

Still another pocket of individuals has refused to acknowledge any of the standard or accepted norms and have pushed for a society that fit their imagined agenda. These individuals seem to have adopted an attitude of... 'I deserve'; and their view of the world may seem to be: rules are for others, but not for me; history has no value; it is my/our turn; and they push forward with a mission lacking any concern for the broader impact.

Then, there is that segment of individuals that has always been focused on creating a new world order that fit their utopian visions. In other words; one that aligns more with their own beliefs and personal values than with what may be for the best and highest good of all at the time. They have even chosen to create roadmaps to accomplish those desires; sometimes in spite of the repercussions for themselves or the world at large. *And, a part of me definitely supports a platform for change and growth!*

However, my style would be to take a pragmatic approach focused on bettering the quality of life for all individuals, communities, businesses, and the society, in general. An approach for change and growth that excludes differing ideas and is seemingly channeled from self-directed emotional energy, may miss the mark in creating a purposeful outcome for the masses. The key mission of **Hello, Self...!**

Regardless, of where you have expressed your humanness, so far in life; saying 'hello' to your genuine self can offer a refreshing new framework for moving forward in creating a screen play and script for the next frame of your life movie.

Now is the time to begin having some serious conversations with self, about those inner most secrets hidden behind the façade that many of us have been living within. There will be some thoughts on the following pages about discovering and uncovering conversations and moments of personal awareness.

However, before we go there, just a reminder that the world of conformity will try to convince you that it is easier to conform than it is to applaud your own personal growth; by recognizing and living your uniqueness. The author below has captured this reality, so eloquently...

**"BEING UNIQUE IS YOUR GIFT IN LIFE,
BEING ABLE TO MAINTAIN
THAT UNIQUENESS IN A WORLD THAT IS
FOCUSED ON CONFORMING;
IS YOUR CHALLENGE."**

-Author Unknown

_____

*"There is nothing more genuine than breaking
away from the chorus to learn the sound of your
own voice."*
-Po Bronson

_____

IT IS YOUR TIME NOW...

believe it and achieve it!

Frame Six...
CONVERSATIONS WITH SELF

To begin this **SIXTH** movie frame, seems best to highlight some key lyrics from a song that says it so well. It is a song by:

> ***The Brothers Osborne singing duo titled..."Younger Me".***

'Younger Me"
Made it harder than it had to be
Trying hard to dodge my destiny
Would get the best of me.

"Younger Me"
Overthinking, losing sleep at night
Contemplating if it's worth the fight
If he only knew he'd be alright
Yeah, younger me.

Reading these specific lyrics, reminds us that most of our struggles are caused by lack of confidence in our own talents or in just over thinking life.

Our approach to acknowledging who we truly are can become diluted when we begin by trying to figure out who we are in the present, while looking back at our past with regret; and glancing ahead with fearful contemplation of the future.

We are seldom truly present or fully aware of our thoughts and feelings at any moment in time. Such scattered behaviors involving the past, present and future all at one time... dilute the effectiveness of 'in the moment' conversations. It all gets muddled by the confusing voices of regret, denial and fear playing out in our mind at the same time.

Paying attention to what and who you are attracting into your presence can be a clue as to what conversations are going on in your inner self. We attract the favorable and the unfavorable as a result of what we are thinking and saying to ourselves. Who do you have in your tribe right now? Are they a reflection of your past, a snapshot of your present or a glimpse of your future? Or all of these.

The company we keep is only one aspect of life that can impact our future success. Another, and perhaps the biggest issue to what holds us back from moving forward, is our conscious or unconscious self speech. Self speech is what we mentally say to ourselves and to others about ourselves.

Your speech can create your self-fulfilling prophecy. You speak about what you are and you become it… for better or worse.

Some of that self speech can become your own self labels, such as: "I'm not smart enough", "I'm not talented"; "My teacher was right, I'll never amount to a hill of beans"; "I'm not athletic"; "I'm not lucky"; "I'm not attractive"; and on and on it continues. You can fill in the rest by similar labels you may have said to yourself.

The above statements are only a fraction of the negative things we say to ourselves each day; either verbally or unconsciously. You could probably list many pages of your own limiting self speech comments; again, some conscious and some unconscious.

In this wonderful world in which we live, it's amazing how very few people truly like themselves. Their self speech defines them, just as surely as it defines their reality. Examples:

YOU SAY YOU ARE, AND SO YOU BECOME!

———

YOU SAY YOU CAN'T, AND SO YOU DON'T.

Self-limiting language often comes from early programming or our environment; and may cause doubt and fear whenever we wish to take a leap of faith or risk something. That is the time we pull back into our comfort zone and stay in our self-assigned corral.

These corrals become our safe space; establishing low levels of expectation within and limiting our capabilities, talents and opportunities… thus, validating our self-fulling prophecies.

So, the question for you is, what are you saying about you and to you? Write those comments down on a piece of paper, date the comments and save them in a jar to have as a later reminder when you witness yourself falling into your negative thinking or negative self-talk. Oh, and before tossing those notes into the jar, remember to say "cancel, cancel". Occasionally, you may wish to check your notes and find that as time has passed you have less and less self-demeaning comments.

By doing this simple activity you will most likely find you are already the person you desire to be. It has just been impossible for you to see it through the fog of self-speech you've become comfortable with. It's amazing how very few people truly love themselves.

By beginning to say loving words to ourselves, we can build a more positive relationship; just as with a friend. Friends give support, provide thoughtful ideas, compliment successes and are with us through, the good and tough times. Becoming our own best friend can be about changing our perception of the ego, as 'bad' or 'boastful'.

The Merriam-Webster definition of ego is: 'a reasonable or justifiable sense of one's worth or importance'. An example of using ego in a sentence as a positive is:

I have enough ego that I don't give up easily when trying to win in a contest, competition or accomplishing a life goal.

More about the ego later in this frame; now back to more discussion about the struggles of having conversations with self in a present state of being.

Analyzing the past and contemplating the future while standing in the present is a sign of scattered energies. Scattered energies cause us to spin in confusion; therefore, blocking any insights or recognizing any signs of confirmation and general gut feelings of who we truly are in the present.

Life, for many of us, feels like driving in the dark without headlights *(or a GPS)!* And regardless of age, some things never change. We just keep driving in the dark much of our life.

From time to time, we all may have conversations with our INNER SELF; however, many of those conversations are more critical than positive.

It is my suggestion that you try to keep your inner conversations on a lighter side, most of the time... *that way you may engage on a different emotional level and then, both of you can laugh; when you observe yourself being ridiculous!!!*

Ever laughed at the ridiculous things you say to yourself, how upset you get over the smallest things or noticed the absurd behaviors that come from you in response to certain situations? Learning to check in with self before taking an action may be the best gift you could ever give yourself.

A simple statement to self as a check-in, might be... "Should I do this?" "Would this be for my best and highest good?" "Is this action necessary at this time?" "Will doing this build a trusting relationship?" Just some thoughts for 'thinking before acting'.

Such actions as these can be instrumental in taking your behavior from an emotional response to a purposeful response; and, to one you may not have to regret later. A brief *Hello, Self...* conversation can be a bridge builder!

Just like the song by **Brothers Osborne**, occasionally, we may applaud the way we handled a situation; still at other times we may be critical of our actions and promise SELF never to do or respond in that same manner, ever again. Then, only to find a few weeks later we have broken our promise to self. This so true for all of us; yet, that initial promise may cause us to become more aware.

And, it is important to remember that we will, at times, allow our negative emotions to react first. When that happens, be kind to self... apologize to the receiver; even if the receiver is you.

Being perfect in all we do is not the goal of this book/movie. *Hello, Self...* is about becoming more self aware and making conscious choices from that awareness. It is not suggesting that we become so paranoid about making a decision or saying something that we are hesitant to take any type of action.

Each of us has from time to time had a conversation with self about our behaviors or our responses; and wished we would have acted in a more positive way or made a different decision. When that happens, we should just applaud ourselves, as the good news is, at least, we are aware of it and noticed. And, secondly, the decision made is not a total loss; as we did learn.

Becoming aware of our behaviors and our thinking by having verbal and mental conversations with the inner self indicates that we are, at least, paying attention. The more we pay attention and become conscious of our inner dialogues, behaviors and actions; the better the chances are of shifting from an automatic response to a chosen response.

Like so many great 'self-help' gurus have said, we are evolving souls; our first steps are to awaken the inner self to conscious knowing.

This frame on conversations with self is intended to help us become open to new beginnings in the way we live life. That is not to say it is easy work; as many of us are living our lives in a mostly unconscious or automatic state of presence, and have been for most of our lifetime. One intentional step can bring awareness and awareness can bring change.

*"What we don't know about ourselves is actually
what controls us".*

The above statement has been quoted many times
and now in reflection, it makes so much sense.
And yet, with all our flaws, we are still perfect
beings... always trying to focus on enhancing our
lives and the lives of others, by staying committed
to living for a higher good.

We may already be the person we desire to be. It's
just impossible for us to see it through the self-
speech we may have become accustomed to, up to
this point.

*"All of you are perfect just as you are...
and there is still room for improvement!"*
-Shunryu Suzuki

**A note of warning at this point, or at least a high-
level alert!!!** The ego likes power and control; and
many times, in your conversations with self, the ego
may try to convince you that this self-awareness
stuff is all a silly game.

The fear of you observing your behaviors, questioning your thoughts and finding your inner knowing is sometimes a threat to the ego's power focused aspect. Therefore, that part of ego will try to interfere with any sort of effort exerted toward getting in touch with the real you and discovering your true personal power.

So how does one recognize the impacts, both positive and negative, of the ego in their life?

As we have begun to realize, there are two sides of the ego. We have mentioned earlier in this frame that it can be as simple as a perception definition.

There is the side of "I CAN" driven by the language of the heart; and the side of "I CAN'T" driven by the thoughts and imaginings of the head and/or social drivers.

The "I CAN" language focuses on such ideals as creation, potential, passion, purpose; while the "DOUBT AND FEAR" or "I CAN'T" language leans toward self-competition, comparison, self-doubt, fear and not good enough. The internal knowing or heart can get silenced by the powerful external noise of the head.

While those two definitions highlight a conceptual level understanding; let's look at some specific examples which might be more helpful.

An article from **INC. MAGAZINE** in 2013, written by Shelly Provost titled: **'5 Ways to Distinguish Your Calling from Your EGO'**. It offers some specifics about how to recognize the key desires of the ego-self when focused on power versus the ego-self when in alignment with a higher purpose or calling.

She lays it out from a comparison point of view... first stating the fear or need aspects of the EGO seeking power; followed by the fear or need aspects of a CALLING.

———

EGO fears not having or doing something. CALLING fears not expressing or being something.

EGO needs anxiety to survive. CALLING needs silence to survive.

EGO manifests as burnout. CALLING manifests as fulfillment.

EGO focuses on results. CALLING focuses on process.

EGO wants to preserve self. CALLING wants impact.

A bad day for your ego is a great day for your soul. Jillian Michaels

Other thoughts to add value to this frame's focus…

"A good hockey player plays knows where the puck is. A great hockey player knows where the puck is going to be."
-Wayne Gretzky

"If you don't play to win don't play at all."
-Tom Brady.

"Our thoughts and imaginations are the only real limits to our possibilities."
-Orison Swett Marden

"As you think, so shall you become."
-Bruce Lee

"If you don't like the road you are walking, start paving another…"
-Dolly Parton

"To be proud of your accomplishments and speak complimentary about them, often attracts prejudice, judging and envy. Do it anyway!"
-Patricia Leonard

Everybody wants to be somebody.

Hello, Self...

Frame Seven...
THE COMMITMENTS

"WINNING is not everything--but making the EFFORT to win is."

-Vince Lombardi

This is the frame where the rubber meets the road; making commitments to the self and then putting action to those commitments. John Maxwell said, "If we are not growing today; how can we expect tomorrow to be better?"

Making commitments to explore who we are can feel like trying to defeat a field of giants. Our life and living have become so natural to us that when we finally begin to realize the many areas of our life these commitments can impact, it may seem overwhelming and may cause us to choose to stay in our uncomfortable comfort zone. Even small life changes bring about ripples of responsibility and change in all areas of our life.

Now it is time for a costume change in this scene; so, put on your magician attire. See yourself as a magician making change happen, and truly believe that you hold a magic wand capable of connecting with your inner knowledge and wisdom. Here are some thoughtful 'abracadabras of magic' that may help to keep the magician within energized:

- *Lack and struggle come from limited thinking! Tell yourself you are powerful and talented!*

- *What we focus on will define our journey! Be positive and claim an 'I can', 'I did' outcome!*

- *The destination is not the key point of focus now; the value and joy of the journey is what matters most! Stay in the present!*

- *Our personal celebrations and self-applause are the motivators that move intentions forward. Become your own cheerleader!*

- *A step-a-day helps in keeping questioning and doubt away. Write a positive note to self every day, read it out loud, then drop in a decorative bowl to retrieve later.*

- *Dreams are gifts; not yet wrapped. See your dreams wrapped in shiny paper with a big glitzy bow!*

- *Love yourself; believe in yourself. Look in a mirror every day and say "I love you" to self.*

- *Conversations with God. Every day let God know how grateful you are for everything: health, shelter, vehicle (mine is named Fancy), food, income, family, friends, community, and just all in your life.*

- *It is okay to have no idea of the 'how' for doing something; the 'knowing' it will happen is the key! We do not have to know how it should or will happen... just begin by trusting the magic of the Hello, Self... moment; the rest will evolve.*

- *"Life is a gift, the way we wrap it is our choice.*

- *"There Are No Right or Wrong Roads; Only Choices."*
  -Ordinary Joe

Now that we have some magic dust ideas sprinkled on our commitment wand; it is time to accept the responsibility of becoming present with self in defining the main takeaways from our personal movie. That clarity will lay the groundwork for the scenes that follow.

Creating an outcome that is in alignment with an awakened self may be more difficult at first as our beginning is set in an already existing culture, economy, and global environment. Breaking away from those established structures can sometimes be difficult as many of them are designed to control the process and support conforming.

This is where the scene must shift from a place of fear and doubt to one of confidence, trust and belief; regardless of the odds against receiving a favorable movie review from others. In other words, the relationship developed with self to this point, has transitioned to a new lead role in your present life movie.

The responsibility, in having this lead role of commitment, is to make things happen and create an outcome that does not make excuses or blame others for low box office sales or failures in receiving an award-winning outcome.

Making excuses or getting sidetracked by what Seth Godin, an entrepreneur, best-selling author and speaker, calls wandering around in the digital swamp or any swamp for that matter, can inhibit progress in accomplishing commitments. These diversions are not always productive, he adds, "It doesn't free our imagination; it actually stifles it". To always wade in the swamp of others evaluations can lead to getting eaten by the alligators or catch a swamp related disease of 'maybe someday' fever.

Other conditions or situations that inhibit progress, as highlighted in the previous text, may be from the general messaging we give ourselves, those we receive from others, or the behaviors we get caught up in on a daily basis, such as:

- **Telling ourselves there is really not enough time or I don't have the money right now; or I will do it when the kids grow up or when the money gets better. That unfortunately, is how our life and** dreams get tossed upon that someday shelf.

– Our mind convinces us that we are not good enough, smart enough or talented enough.

– Associating with nay-sayers!

– Speaking self-defeating language in conversations with self and others, such as: "I have a lot of ideas but, don't really know how to get started implementing them" or "I wish I knew how to write a book, but I have nothing interesting to share" or "I wish I could get the energy up to lose some weight" ... but, but, but!

– Getting caught up in the too late for me thinking such as: I am too old... just wish I had thought about this when I was younger... have missed all the opportunity moments while raising family... etc.

– Telling ourselves we doubt if it will work; then, just giving up before we even start.

– One thing to remember: Life isn't all about finding yourself. Life is about creating yourself, too.

Paying attention to the traps we fall into that throw us off track from accomplishing commitments is a key part of maintaining a self-awareness presence. As a matter of fact, this might be a great place to test your personal commitment levels with an assessment of past behaviors, based upon your own self-evaluation. Interested?

If so, here is what you need to do. Below on the **"I" Personality Traits Assessment** place a check mark on the blank line next to the statement that best describes a trait you see in yourself.

"I" Personality Traits Assessment
(Not a scientific based assessment, unless you are a scientist ☺!)

_____I seldom give up on goals or projects once I commit.

_____I am a procrastinator; put things off.

_____I schedule calendar time for what I want to get done. And I do it.

_____I do what I say I will do; even when committing to myself.

_____I plan and follow through on 'me time' every day.

_____I am easily swayed by others.

_____I am a leader and I take charge of my goals and dreams.

_____I have a history of dropping the ball when things go wrong.

_____I start with a lot of energy and halfway through I lose it.

_____I welcome feedback and ask for advice.

_____I have a lot to juggle right now… there seems too always be something.

_____I declare that this is my year!

_____I am too old to start something new.

_____I see through barriers and hurdles to possibilities.

_____I have encouragers in my tribe to keep me on target.

_____I believe in myself and my talents.

_____I am my own cheerleader.

_____I am impulsive.

_____I listen to my heart; more than my head.

_____I am courageous and a risk taker.

_____I struggle with and get frustrated when what I plan gets disrupted.

_____I am guilty of helping others and delaying my own needs.

_____I practice doing something positive for others every day.

_____This is not a good time in my life to start something.

_____I give myself daily affirmations.

_____I am a *'go with the flow'* type person.

_____I should wait until I retire. I would have more time then.

_____I get impatient for results.

_____I am too busy with family and job at this time.

_____I start with lots of excitement and get easily distracted by other things.

_____I am more focused on my needs NOW; than ever in my life.

_____I believe in ME!

Now that the assessment has been taken; circle those that could inhibit you from manifesting your goals and commitments *(make no excuses for any traits circled)!*

Based upon your own personal personality traits assessment; is there some work yet to be done to ensure you will be ready to move forward on manifesting any commitments you make to yourself? If so, take care of those things now; if not, this brings us to the next frame of this life book/movie, which requires you going from talking to walking on pledges you have made; or will be making. A couple of reminders follow:

"I am learning every day
to allow the space
between where I am
and where I want to be
to inspire me and not
terrify me."

- Tracee Ellis Ross

THERE MAY NEVER BE A PERFECT TIME FOR

SOME PEOPLE, AS SEEN THROUGH THEIR

EYES. ARE YOU ONE OF THEM?

Hello, Self...

Frame Eight...
MANIFESTATION

FRAME EIGHT of our **Hello, Self...** book/movie stresses that once we have built a relationship and personal understanding of the values and vision of self; made a commitment to take the action necessary to implement; it then becomes the time to plan for that journey. Below are some energizing words from Lou Holz, to jumpstart that effort.

"Ability is what you're capable of doing. Motivation determines what you will do. Attitude determines how well you do it."

It makes sense at this point to restate the intended mission in writing this book. The goals were and are about... *manifesting and living our lives with awareness of who we are in the present moment.*

So, saying hello to self, having conversations with self and evaluating one's commitment levels, are great first steps to manifesting and living life on purpose.

However; conversation, discovery and commitment to make a difference do not guarantee implementation. Just because we have laid the groundwork, completed some activities focused on expanding our knowing and learning; and made a pledge to follow through on that awareness, does not guarantee the action will happen!

Words are not action; they only speak intended action.

Manifestation is about exhibiting or displaying a result. For example, Christopher Priest, a British Novelist and a Science Fiction Writer and author of "THE PRESTIGE" tells a story of two feuding magicians at the turn of the century. Christopher says, that every magic trick consists of three stages for manifestation.

The first stage he calls 'the pledge'... *stating what the magic will be.*

...Example: I will cause a rabbit to jump out of a hat.

———

The second stage he defines as 'the turn' which is about taking action on the pledge.

...Example: Says some magic words over a hat and manifests the pledge made; by causing a rabbit to jump out of the hat.

———

The third stage he identifies is 'the prestige' which is about gracefully accepting the approval feedback when the audience watches in awe; then applauds with recognition.

...Example: Taking a bow after an applause of approval and recognition from an audience for the success.

———

This three-step process is applicable for creating magic in all goals undertaken. These three words define manifestation... **Commit, Act** and **Receive.**

Following, are some thoughts as an example of what *Frame Eight* of the movie/book is expected to demonstrate based up Christopher Priest's descriptions of the three phases.

The first stage in Hello, Self... *committing to reveal the real self through conversations with self.*

The second stage in Hello, Self... *defining and clarifying the specifics of one's commitment to self-discovery; then creating the roadmap for action.*

The third stage in Hello. Self... *manifesting results; then honoring and celebrating self for taking the actions necessary to create an ongoing magical and purposeful life experience.*

Whether you see yourself as a Merlin or not is insignificant. What is important is to believe you have the ability to manifest your dreams and goals; and that celebrating your accomplishments are motivating.

We each like an applause; and perhaps the most important applause comes from self. It can be the catalyst that inspires one to create more magic in their life. We all like successful outcomes!

———

"To be yourself in a world that is constantly trying to make you something else is the greatest accomplishment."

-Ralph Waldo Emerson

———

'To Thine Own Self Be True'

*This is a line from **Shakespeare's play, Hamlet**. It is spoken by King Claudius' chief minister, Polonius as part of a speech he is giving his son, Laertes,*
his blessing and advice on how to behave whilst at university;
and is so appropriate here.

Frame Nine...

CELEBRATION

Hello, Self... from a past reflection, can be about celebrating the moments in life that made us who we are today. What have been some **Hello Self...** moments that have changed your life significantly?

FRAME NINE is the part of your life book/movie that gives you goose bumps or causes tears to well up in your eyes and fills your heart with celebration of who you are, who you have become and who you are becoming!

This frame is not an ending; it is the beginning of a life that respects celebration of self and acknowledges that each of us; yes, even you, have a desire to be celebrated. For celebration of yourself to be truly valued and impactful; it must first come from you.

The act of 'self-celebration' has been something that our society has seen as an ego power celebration rather than an act of self love. That society norm has turned us into feeling ego centered from a negative point of view; if we applaud our accomplishments. It is time for that to change… there is a difference between applauding self, having pride in self; celebrating self; and self centered bragging, gloating, arrogance or conceitedness.

This writing and your reading this book have no value if you buy into the belief that 'self celebration' is boastful and solely ego power centered; and deny yourself the honor of loving you and celebrating you.

Learning to love yourself is really one of the key reason 'WHY' this book/movie can offer value to you, the reader. When we feel free that we can truly be who we desire to be without fear of being misunderstood, judged, or sounding conceited; we can then be free to express.

Wearing societal masks of fitting in, being part of a certain group think, or denying self of expression based upon fear of not using the appropriate language or abiding by the new society definitions, dressing according to a certain age appropriate couture, laughing at jokes that may be offensive (*to someone!!!*), or being labeled by society as a misfit, or not having a positive image about self; because you are afraid of repercussions. Oh, we could go on and on with examples; but there is some space below where so you can add your own!!!

WRITE DOWN WHY WE AS INDIVIDUALS CONTINUE TO WEAR MASKS TO HIDE WHO WE TRULY ARE.

(And this is not speaking about physical masks; but the invisible masks of pretense, escape or disguise.)

_____

_____

_____

_____

_____

_____

_____

_____

_____

_____

_____

_____

_____

_____

_____

_____

_____

_____

...of creating yourself.

_____

Life is about learning and celebrating self!

_____

At this point in our book/movie it may make sense to expand our view of personal celebration and recognition by examining what others have said about acknowledging, praising, toasting and speaking 'self-celebration words'... and any other ways of applauding self.

Life isn't about finding yourself. Life is about creating yourself!

_____

Love makes the world go around and it starts first with self-love.

"Love Can Build a Bridge"
as expressed by the Judd's song

"Be yourself no matter what they say!"
-Sting

"Celebrations infuse life with passion and purpose. They summon the human spirit."
-Terrence E. Deal

"Celebration has many different outfits but she always wears the same beautiful dancing shoes."
-Mary Anne Radmacher

"Share our similarities, celebrate our differences."
-M. Scott Peck

"Courage is like a muscle. We strengthen it with use."
-Ruth Gordon

"All that is wrapped in love and tied with a big glitzy bow will result in magical outcomes. Celebrate your total package!"
-Patricia Leonard

Hello, Self...

Key Takeaways...

REVIEW

Life can become richer and more meaningful when we take the time to have conversations with self; about self; and, in general, get to know who we really are! This consciousness brings the opportunity for living life in alignment with soul purpose.

Once the window to self-conversation is opened, you will be surprised at how the interaction between the inner you and the outer you will expand your awarensss.

This relationship creates the opportunity for establishing our choices and emotions about how we respond to all aspects of our life. Believe it or not... how we feel about ourself has a lot to do with our perception of situations and people; and impacts the way we respond to them.

Ever experienced individuals who seem to have an 'angry' on a lot of the time? Well, if you could see under that non-physical mask they are wearing, you might see that there exists a person who has a low self-image, feels powerless and sees themselves 'less than' in some aspect of their life. How sad!

Conversations with self may surface varying realizations, some with meaningful discoveries; others bringing forth new choices and emotional responses. Some may even cause us to scold ourselves or find humor in who we are and the way we behave!

Regardless of your approach to self; be kind and remember you are a soul on a journey titled 'learning as you go'. You may say to yourself that you do not have the time to have conversations with self or engage in any of this craziness about getting to know yourself. The benefits from this work will offer many more blessings than what could be measured on your cellphones calculators.

SOME THOUGHTS TO PONDER
ABOUT CONVERSATIONS WITH SELF:

———————

"Loving yourself isn't vanity. It's sanity."
-Katrina Mayer

———————

"Lighten up on yourself. No one is perfect.
Gently accept your humanness."
-Deborah Day

———————

"Arguments always begin with an answer in
mind. Conversation begins with a question."
-Unknown

———————

"Maybe saying 'YES' more often can help us discover more of who we are!!!"
-Unknown

———————

"Without the ability to end things, people stay stuck, never becoming who they are meant to be, never accomplishing all that their talents and abilities should afford them."
-Dr. Henry Cloud

———————

"If you don't love yourself, nobody will. Not only that, you won't be good at loving anyone else. Loving starts with the self."
-Wayne Dyer

———————

"Who looks outside, dreams; who looks inside, awakes."
-Carl Gustav Jung

———————

"The reward for conformity is that everyone likes you, but yourself."
-Rita Mae Brown

———————

"When you lose yourself, you find your key to paradise."
-Line from a Chris Stapleton song

"Be who you are and say what you feel, because those who mind don't matter, and those who matter don't mind.
So…
Learn to love yourself; even your flaws and imperfections."
-Dr. Seuss

"Do not conform to the pattern of this world, but be transformed by the renewing of your mind."
-Romans 12:2

"Being unique is your gift in life, being able to maintain that uniqueness in a world that is focused on conforming, is your challenge!"
-Author Unknown

"Courage begets courage."
-Ruth Gordon

"As we age, we have the opportunity to discover our deeper essence beyond the body and express our inner."
-Eckhart Tolle

"He who wants a rose must respect the thorn."
-Persian Proverb

---

*"The roads not seen almost always matter more than the potholes
we hit along the way."*
-Seth Godin

"Letting go is an art of far greater power than defending or hanging on."
-Eckhart Tolle

"Sometimes, things work the way they are supposed to, even if it's not what we might want in the moment."
-Seth Godin

"Sometimes when we talk to ourselves, we both may laugh!!!"
-Unknown

"There is pleasure in the pathless woods."
-Lord Byron

*(The above quote is from a tea bag label I discovered while sipping a cup of tea.
Life gives us gifts no matter where we are.)*

---

*"Nature does not hurry,
yet everything is accomplished."*
-LAO TZU

ALWAYS REMEMBER ... *you are enough,
just as you are!*

From the Author...
CLOSING NOTES

Interesting note about my own learning while writing this book/movie. As the thoughts, words and expressions surfaced; a realization occurred... it is a book where my life and personal awareness begin to unfold right in front of me; almost as if I, too, was creating a movie of my own personal profile... just as I have been asking you to do as you read the pages.

Everything, in some way, reflects my life history and experiences, as well as the journeys of others who have been willing to share with me, their own adventures during our coaching and workshop sessions. It is now even more clear that one person's sharing is not only a reflection of themselves; but, also, often a mirror image of others. Are we really more alike than we are different?

Interestingly enough, it is often said that songwriters, authors, speakers, etc., write about and talk about what they have experienced, need to learn or are going through in their own lives. Well, that statement fits in this circumstance, as writing this book has definitely been a transitioning time for me, personally. And, I trust that you reading it will prove to be true for you.

Having said that, it seems the appropriate time now to share how the title of this movie/book arrived; and give credit where credit is due.

For months, I had been spinning in my own thoughts about my next life or career step; by asking myself out loud, "What is next for me?" I even engaged in a conversation with God, about the same question.

It was early one morning just before awakening that a booming voice said, "Patricia, just use, hello self." It appeared that booming voice was adamant about getting my attention and obviously a little frustrated after having no success previously; so, decided to up the volume… which definitely got my attention!

Being shocked by the clarity and volume of the voice; my immediate response was a question... "What is hello self?" Then when no response came, I went on with my day; continually being reminded of the words and the commitment in the voice. It appears there are times in our life when the soul and human self become like two ships passing in the night; unaware of the other's presence, therefore; unable to hear or connect.

The meaning of the words haunted me, and yet; rang true as an appropriate description of my personal feelings while trying to find direction in the unstable times of a national and global health epidemic. Getting to know self, somehow, seemed an important step in helping myself and others create some sense of balance.

Those major changes at the introduction of a new decade, had tossed people into a totally unfamiliar environment where nothing was truly stable or reflected much of what had previously been called 'normal life'. Of course, change happens, that is guaranteed; yet, the recent changes had been magnified by taking place in multiple segments of the society and the world; simultaneously.

Feeling a sense of control and acceptance can be a very powerful motivator in a transitioning life, society, culture and world community. The intention with **Hello, Self...** was to provide that motivation by encouraging you, in expanding your personal visions, building runways to success and becoming instrumental in stimulating your own boldness in living a fulfilled life.

As earlier stated, Dr. Stephen Covey, says that self work must start with first knowing self; defining the present situation as experienced or perceived by self; acknowledging the talents of self and clarifying intended goals.

Starting with self from where we are, is necessary to finding balance in an unbalanced world. Perhaps finding balance is more about an individual finding their voice and using that voice in speaking positively to self about self... as well as sharing it with others as has been the case with this writing.

As we have continued to emphasize, the global world is in transition; *(as always of course, but we are now paying more attention, it seems...)* which is a perfect time to clarify the real SELF! Now is the time to personalize one's own desires for living a fulfilled and happy life and clearing a path on the road ahead.

As the world changes, truths change; our truths change! Be willing to be inquisitive and be willing to accept the conclusions that your senses provide even if, they contradict hard won beliefs within you. Be curious, and open to learning and gaining new perspectives by understanding situations from differing viewpoints.

Your choices are important in framing your life and future. And remember, your choices in one area will always cause ripples in many directions, making an impact in various other areas of your living. Choose wisely!

"Life is a gift; the way you wrap it is truly your choice."

You are the actor, director, producer, viewer; and reviewer, of your own life movie! May it become an Oscar winning production; by you and for you!

AND NOW, THIS SPECIAL AWARD GOES

TO YOU FOR YOUR

PERFORMANCE IN THE

Hello, Self...

***BOOK*/MOVIE!!!**

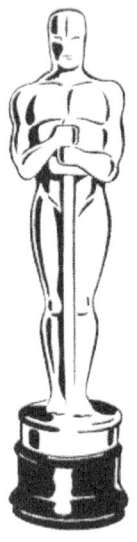

Congratulations!!!

FINAL THOUGHTS

Other interesting ways
To connect with self...

Are you ready to do something else. Just for fun?

As we have intimated earlier, connection with self is much more than speaking a language of words. As a matter of fact, the lack of words is often the most powerful and meaningful conversations with self. Are you ready to have a wordless conversation with yourself? If so, here is an artistic activity for you to try.

Get a canvas, brush and paints, then find a quiet place; maybe out of doors or in a room where you are alone and perhaps have music playing. Do not be afraid to engage in the exercise; because you think you are not an artist.

This is about creating a visual of who you are…trusting whatever comes will be your soul's expression…without evaluating the outcome as if you are an art critic.

The result may not be a human form, or a specific form of any type. Let your inner self just express through feelings, emotions, thoughts, silence and nothingness.

This activity is not about being an artist; but being a free spirit engaging the help of a brush, paint colors and inner dialogue of your subjective reality through the feelings and emotions of the soul and body... and not through the objective reality of the five senses of sight, hearing, touch, taste and smell.

It is about allowing your inner self to express whatever comes through with the paint brush strokes and colors you choose. It is not about taking something from a picture, or listening to your ego about how it looks, should look or trying to figure out what to express at that moment.

So often in life, self sends us a message and we ignore it because it does not fit our rigidly established lifestyle or picture of who we are or how we look; this is not one of those times.

We often compare our soul expressions based upon a narrowly defined blueprint of some person or society with the answers... this is the time to express your life outside the box of expert expectations, society norms and ego comparisons.

To truly let go and trust self is often scary; since most of us have lived in a façade afraid of letting the world see our fears, doubts, and core self. Most deny themselves personal expression by hiding under the cover of titles, education, social status, material assets, and well, you get the picture.

Are you ready to reveal your real self and release the burdens of a façade? Authenticity is the best gift you can give yourselves and; authenticity is the best gift you can give the world.

Hang this finished art piece in your office or home where you and others can view it. It may be interesting to experience the conversations that surface from and with others... as well as with yourself!

When viewing your artistic expression over time see if the image changes meaning for you; what other details begin to stand out; the significance of the paint colors chosen; the size of the art piece and the various conversations it stimulates.

This can be used as a group or team building activity too, creating an art piece with each member adding a unique artistic expression of their personal experience in being part of the group or team.

After completion, the art piece can then be hung in a visible location, as a reminder of the diverse experiences of each individual, working in the same group or team. It can be a great way to measure progress and growth by referring back periodically and engaging in a group conversation about any new views of the painting.

As new team members are brought on board; they can be introduced to the art piece and its value for the group; and for the leadership.

Another, 'conversation with self' idea.

Ask yourself what type of shoe is most like your personality? Here are some shoe samples and suggested traits to get you started.

Stiletto  *Italian Word 'stiletto'' meaning 'dagger'.*

...Like to feel sexy and feminine!

...Impatient with others. Sharp tongue!

...Take control; see self as a leader.

...Risk taker... rises above the muck of life!

...Likes a feeling of importance and status!

PLATFORM SHOE

...A comedian, Pee Wee Herman, type!

...Having a solid foundation is very important!

...Seeks security; not a risk taker.

...Stays out of the dirty laundry & gossip in life!

...Rises above a negative situation; finds a higher good.

BALLERINA DANCING SHOE

...Dances around issues, trying to please everyone.

…Thinks of self as a 'Prima-Donna'; special.

…Tiptoes into commitments.

…Once in, is committed and dedicated.

…Quiet type - actions speak louder than words.

FLIP FLOPS

…Has a difficult time making decisions.

…Makes a decision then doubts self.

…Changes mind often.

…Has laidback attitude of 'I will do it someday'.

…Resists the uncomfortable and confining.

SANDALS

…Is a free spirit; does it their way.

…Sometimes seen as a loner…likes space.

…Individual – not controlled by others.

…Appreciates an outdoor concert over a theater.

…Not interested in fancy clothes.

…Chooses comfort over aesthetics.

SNEAKERS

...Seeks comfort over style.

...Agreeable; finds consensus.

...Game player.

...Laid back attitude.

...Slow to disclose.

...Unexpected responses.

LOW HEEL PUMPS

...High self-confidence. Grounded.

...In charge type.

...Can be intimating.

...Prefers to keep thoughts secret/private.

...Takes care of business, gets it done!

...Finds middle ground approaches.

COWBOY/COWGIRL

...Outdoors and rugged type.

...Statement maker. This is me!

...Comfort versus style.

...No pretense lifestyle.

...Likes old western movies.

...No frills living.

Now create your own shoe type persona here; or ask another person to create it for you! This can also be a fun group or organization activity to do and share with each member.

What is the SHOE PERSONALITY TITLE and the associated GRAPHIC; then define the traits?

...Trait

...Trait

...Trait

...Trait

...Trait

...Trait

When participating in this activity, the question of whether one can fit into multiple shoe types invariably comes up. And the answer is, of course… as the idea is not to box a person into being a certain type only, as we are all diverse individuals.

It is for fun and, again, an opportunity for discovering self through another avenue. The intent is to simply offer a way to stay mindful of who we are in a given moment, in a given day, in a challenging event, or in a multitude of situations we may find ourselves encountering. It is a way we can define our feelings, emotions and behaviors in our everyday lives or in a specific situation.

Example: This week you may be a platform rising above the muck of gossip going on; or you are ready for the party feel of the stiletto; or, it is a sneaker day of relaxing.

It is simply a way of understanding and honoring self on a given day; instead of beating oneself up for being or feeling different, out of sorts, or lethargic; just learning to acknowledge the inner and outer selves simultaneously without judgement.

Hello Self... is about revealing self to self. The revealing process can happen and does happen in many ways; once we commit to paying attention to our emotions, thoughts and behaviors in the present moment... with an intention of improving our quality of living.

One more way to learn more about self is to have a group conversation which can be a lot of fun and eye opening, too. See below:

- Cut strips of paper

- On each strip of paper write a personality trait or any word

- Toss the strips of paper in a box or bowl

- Have each person in the group draw a strip of paper, at random

- Ask each individual to share what they think the word they drew says about them

- Next have the group share their view of how that person's word defines their view of the individual's personality or personal traits; based upon their experience of that person. (*Be kind*).

REMEMBER THIS ACTIVITY IS TO BE FUN AND
EXPAND OUR AWARENESS OF SELF...
AND
OFFER A CONSTRUCTIVE VIEW OF ANOTHER;
NOT A DESTRUCTIVE VIEW!

HAVE FUN AND LEARN; OR DON'T

PARTICIPATE!

(p.s. You will learn more about yourself and your perceptions and biases... secretly kept, of course.)

*The final thought of this segment is intended to highlight that any and every experience in our lives can become **a Hello, Self...** moment if we engage in it from that viewpoint.*

THIS IS A WRAP...

THE LIGHTS ARE UP AND THE BOOK/MOVIE IS OVER!

Toss the empty popcorn boxes and soda cans, then relax a few minutes while contemplating your journey in this book/movie, by reviewing the key parts that remain vividly planted in your mind.

The book/movie's closing music comes from these words in a Michael Jackson song ...

'MAN IN THE MIRROR'

"I'm gonna make a change ...
I'm starting with the man in the mirror
I'm asking him to change his ways
And no message could've been any clearer
If you 'wanna' make the world a better place
Take a look at yourself and then make that change".

Final reminder...

*A cloud does not know
why it moves in such a
direction and at such a speed,*

*It feels an impulsion... this is
the place to go now. But the sky knows
the reasons and the patterns
behind all clouds,*

*and you will know, too, when
you lift yourself high enough
to see beyond
horizons.*

*This is from...ILLUSIONS
The Adentures Of A Reluctant Messiah*

by

Richard Bach

THE END AND THE BEGINNING! "

YOU ARE WORTH IT!

A Blank page for your

Hello Self...

thoughts/notes …

Made in the USA
Coppell, TX
15 July 2022